What is "GRACE"?

THE BEST DEFINITION THAT BIBLE THEOLOGIANS HAVE BEEN ABLE TO COME UP WITH IS THAT GOD'S "GRACE" IS **UNMERITED FAVOR!** "UNMERITED" MEANS IT'S SOMETHING WE DON'T REALLY DESERVE, BUT GOD GIVES IT TO US.

ALL OF US ARE SINNERS, AND IT IS GOD'S **GRACE** THAT ENABLES US TO BE SAVED — WITHOUT GOD'S GRACE WE WOULD ALL BE HOPELESSLY **LOST!**

GOD'S GRACE IS A **FREE GIFT** TO MANKIND, AND IT IS AVAILABLE TO ANY HONEST-HEARTED PERSON WHO CRIES OUT TO GOD FOR HELP!

GRACE

FRIENDS, HERE COMES THE REASON FOR DOING THIS BOOK:

THERE ARE SOME CHRISTIANS WHO THINK THAT GOD'S LAW HAS BEEN "CANCELLED" JUST BECAUSE **ROMANS 6:14** TELLS US THAT WE ARE "*NOT UNDER THE LAW, BUT UNDER GRACE*"...

3

PART 1 — "The LAW"

THE FIRST THING WE NEED TO DO IS UNDERSTAND WHAT "THE LAW" IS, AND IT'S NOT QUITE AS SIMPLE AS YOU MIGHT THINK!

WHEN "THE LAW" IS MENTIONED IN THE BIBLE, SOMETIMES THE JEWISH WRITERS WERE REFERRING TO THE **PENTATEUCH**, THE FIRST **5** BOOKS OF THE BIBLE, AND AT OTHER TIMES THEY WERE REFERRING ONLY TO THE **10 COMMANDMENT LAW**, AND/OR THE **CEREMONIAL LAW**, ETC..! ALL OF THESE LAWS ARE UNIQUELY DISTINCT AND DIFFERENT LAWS — AND WE **MUST** BE ABLE TO DISCERN THEM ONE FROM ANOTHER!

TO BEGIN WITH, IS EVERYONE AWARE THAT **MOSES** WENT UP ON MOUNT SINAI **SEVERAL TIMES**? AND MOSES BROUGHT BACK A TOTAL OF

4 DIFFERENT SETS OF LAWS!

AND HERE THEY ARE!

#1 The Moral Law

The Ten Commandments, written by God on stone tablets!

Exodus 20:1-17

#2 The Civil Law

Moses wrote these laws on a scroll!

(Exodus 24:4)

Exodus 21-23

"And Mount Sinai was altogether on a smoke, because the Lord descended upon it in *fire...*"

Exodus 19:18

Judges 5:5
Hebrews 12:18

I am the Lord thy God...

Exodus 20:1

#3 The Ceremonial Law

The sacrificial system, and the yearly Sabbath feasts!

Leviticus 1-7, 23:4-44

#4 The Health Law

The dietary laws, and various counsels for good health!

Leviticus 11:1 - 15:33

MOSES at Mt.SINAI

THE YEAR WAS ABOUT *1446 B.C.*, AND GOD GAVE MOSES THE INSTRUCTIONS TO BUILD A *TABERNACLE* FOR HIM TO DWELL IN, AND VARIOUS PIECES OF FURNITURE — THE MOST IMPORTANT BEING THE ARK OF THE COVENANT !

THE *TEN COMMANDMENT STONES* THAT WERE WRITTEN WITH GOD'S OWN FINGER WERE PLACED *INSIDE* THE ARK, AND THE SCROLL ("BOOK") WHEREIN MOSES HAD WRITTEN DOWN THE FIRST *5 BOOKS* OF THE BIBLE (*Genesis, Exodus, Leviticus, Numbers, Deuteronomy*) WAS PLACED IN A POCKET ON THE "SIDE" OF THE ARK, NOT IN THE BOX PORTION OF THE ARK — A VERY IMPORTANT DISTINCTION !

Deuteronomy 31:24-26

MOSES' BROTHER *AARON* WAS ANOINTED AS HIGH PRIEST, AND THE MEN OF THE TRIBE OF *LEVI* BECAME THOSE WHO WOULD OVERSEE THE DAILY MINISTRATIONS OF THE TABERNACLE AND THE ANIMAL SACRIFICES, ALL OF WHICH WERE "SHADOWS" THAT POINTED TOWARDS THE ULTIMATE SACRIFICE OF *JESUS/YESHUA*, THE *LAMB OF GOD* !

GOD'S PRESENCE EVENTUALLY MOVED OFF OF *MT. SINAI* (*God had descended upon the mount in smoke and fire, His presence "melted" and "burned to blackness" the top of the mountain; see Judges 5:5 and Hebrews 12:18*), AND THEN THE *SHEKINAH GLORY* OF GOD TOOK RESIDENCE IN THE *MOST HOLY* COMPARTMENT OF THE TABERNACLE !

SIDE NOTE:

The Ark represented the throne of God, and angels do _not_ belong "on" God's throne — that is why I have drawn the two Cherubim on the sides of the Ark. Others have rendered them this way, so this is not a "new" idea.

7

HERE'S A RATHER SCARY BIBLE VERSE...

" For the time will come when they will **not endure sound doctrine** ... ... and they shall *turn* away their ears from the *Truth*! "

2 Timothy 4: 3-4

THE BIBLE WARNS US THAT IN THE "END TIMES" THAT PEOPLE WILL BE **LAZY** STUDENTS OF THE BIBLE — AND THEY WILL WANT "SMOOTH THINGS" PREACHED TO THEM. *

THE TRUTH OF THE MATTER IS THIS:

OUR ETERNAL SALVATION HINGES UPON UNDERSTANDING "SOUND DOCTRINE"!

*Isaiah 30:10

PART 2

PETER'S *WARNING*
ABOUT PAUL'S WRITINGS *!*

PAUL WROTE _14_ OF THE **27** BOOKS OF THE BIBLE'S NEW TESTAMENT ...

PETER KNEW THAT PAUL WROTE SOME THINGS THAT WERE "HARD TO BE UNDERSTOOD," AND PEOPLE WHO WERE "UNLEARNED" AND "UNSTABLE" WOULD BE PRONE TO

TWIST PAUL'S WORDS "UNTO THEIR OWN *DESTRUCTION*"!

2nd Peter 3:15,16

GOD *KNEW* THAT THERE WOULD BE CERTAIN "PROBLEMS" WITH PEOPLE MISINTERPRETING SOME OF PAUL'S WRITINGS, *AND IT'S STILL HAPPENING !*

READ ON, AND PLEASE REALIZE THAT IT'S VERY IMPORTANT FOR US TO *UNDERSTAND* WHAT PAUL HAS WRITTEN ...

The Big Question

DID PAUL WRITE AND SAY THAT GOD'S LAW WAS "CANCELLED"?

"Do we then make void the law through faith? God forbid: yea, we *establish* the law."

Romans 3:31

"For not the hearers of the law are just before God, but the *doers* of the law shall be justified."

Romans 2:13

"Wherefore the *law* is holy, and the *commandment* holy, and just, and *good.*"

Romans 7:12

"For I *delight* in the *law of God...*"

Romans 7:22

IT IS QUITE OBVIOUS FROM READING THESE TEXTS THAT PAUL **NEVER** MEANT FOR PEOPLE TO THINK THAT "THE LAW" WAS GONE.

PAUL DID HIS BEST TO EXPLAIN THE RELATIONSHIP OF "LAW" TO "GRACE," AND IT ISN'T A SIMPLE THING TO DO. BUT THE FACT IS THAT *BOTH* EXIST!

BOTH!

HERE IS ONE OF THE MOST MISUNDERSTOOD VERSES IN THE BIBLE:

"For Christ is *the end of the law* for righteousness to every one that believeth."

Romans 10:4

IS PAUL SAYING THAT CHRIST *"ended the law"*?

NO, HE'S NOT!

HERE IS HOW THE *JEWISH NEW TESTAMENT* TRANSLATES THIS VERSE:

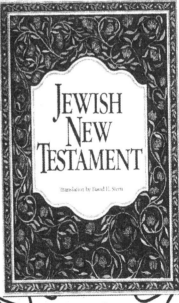

JEWISH NEW TESTAMENT

Translation by David H. Stern

"For *the goal at which the Torah aims* is the Messiah, who offers righteousness to everyone who trusts."

THIS TRANSLATION IS MUCH BETTER!

CHRIST **NEVER** *"ENDED"* THE LAW!

Think not that I am come to destroy the law, or the prophets:

I am not come to destroy, but to **fulfil!**

For verily I say unto you, Till **heaven and earth pass, one jot or one tittle shall in no wise pass from the law,** till all be fulfilled.

QUESTION: JESUS SAID IN MATTHEW 5:17-18 THAT HE CAME TO "*FULFIL*" THE LAW — DOES THIS MEAN JESUS CAME TO "*END*" THE LAW?

NO!

THE GREEK WORD " αναπληρωσατε " (FULFIL) DOES **NOT** MEAN "TO END," BUT "*TO FILL TO ITS FULLEST*" OR TO "*PERFECT*"!

THE FOLLOWING VERSES CONTAIN THE WORD "FULFIL" — TRY SUBSTITUTING THE WORD "END" AND SEE IF THESE VERSES STILL MAKE SENSE:

COL 1:25 *"Whereof I am made a minister, according to the dispensation of God which is given to me for you, to fulfil the word of God;"* (End the word of God?)

COL 4:17 *"And say to Archippus, Take heed to the ministry which thou hast received in the Lord, that thou fulfil it."* (End the ministry?)

2TH 1:11 *"Wherefore also we pray always for you, that our God would count you worthy of this calling, and fulfil all the good pleasure of his goodness, and the work of faith with power:"* (End the good pleasure of God?)

MAT 5:17 *"Think not that I am come to destroy the law, or the prophets: I am not come to destroy, but to fulfil."* (To end the law?)

MAT 3:15 *"And Jesus answering said unto him, Suffer it to be so now: for thus it becometh us to fulfil all righteousness."* (To end all righteousness?)

PHI 2:2 *"Fulfil ye my joy, that ye be likeminded, having the same love, being of one accord, of one mind."* (End ye my joy?)

GAL 6:2 *"Bear ye one another's burdens, and so fulfil the law of Christ."* (End the law of Christ?)

IT IS VERY APPARENT THAT "TO END" WAS *NOT* THE INTENT OF THESE BIBLE VERSES!

THE VERY NEXT VERSE IN MATTHEW CONTAINS WHAT WE CAN CALL

A _VERY_ SERIOUS WARNING :

"... Whosoever therefore shall _break_ one of these least commandments, and _shall_ _teach men so,_ he shall be called the _least_ in the kingdom of heaven."

Matthew 5:19

THIS IS A STRAIGHT-FORWARD **WARNING** FOR US!

WE ARE _NOT_ TO TEACH THAT JESUS "CANCELLED" THE LAW!

WHAT WOULD HAPPEN IF PEOPLE TAUGHT THAT **GOD'S LAW** WAS NO LONGER INTACT NOR IMPORTANT? _PEOPLE WOULD BE EFFECTIVELY TEACHING THAT IT'S "OK" TO_

BREAK GOD'S LAW!

AND _SIN!_

AND THERE'S _NO WAY_ THAT GOD WOULD AGREE TO THAT.

15

"There is therefore now *no condemnation* to them which are in Christ Jesus ... For the law of the Spirit of life in Christ Jesus hath made me *free from the law of sin and death.*"

Romans 8:1-2

IS THIS VERSE SAYING THAT THE CHRISTIAN IS "FREE AND CLEAR" OF BEING HELD RESPONSIBLE FOR SINNING? *NO WAY!* PAUL IS TELLING US THAT THERE IS NO CONDEMNATION FOR THOSE WHO ARE *TRULY* CONVERTED AND "BORN AGAIN" —— AND THIS CONDITION NEEDS TO BE CAREFULLY WATCHED AND DEVELOPED! IF A PERSON ONLY HAS A "LUKEWARM" CONVERSION, HERE'S WHAT GOD SAYS HE WILL DO:

"Because thou art lukewarm, and neither hot nor cold, I will spue thee out of my mouth!"

Revelation 3:16

"LAZY" PEOPLE MAKE "LAZY" WORKERS, AND NOBODY APPRECIATES *LAZY WORKERS* —

IT'S THE SAME WAY WITH GOD — HE DOES *NOT* APPROVE OF SLOTHFUL, "LAZY" BEHAVIOR IN HIS CHRISTIANS!

A CHRISTIAN IS SUPPOSED TO KEEP GOD FIRST AND FOREMOST IN THEIR DAILY LIFE, AND JESUS SAID, "HE THAT ENDURETH TO THE END SHALL BE SAVED!"

Matthew 10:22

THIS IS WHAT GOD REQUIRES OF US — TOTAL COMMITMENT!

PART 3 — GOD'S GRACE

"LAW" AND "GRACE" **BOTH** EXIST!

THE TRICK IS LEARNING TO HAVE A **BALANCED UNDERSTANDING** OF HOW THEY INTERRELATE TO EACH OTHER — AND ONE OF THE SIMPLIEST WAYS TO DO THIS IS TO USE THE ILLUSTRATION OF A **ROW BOAT.**

LAW ... GRACE

IF YOU WERE IN THAT ROW BOAT AND ONLY USED **ONE** OF YOUR OARS, YOU'D MERELY END UP ROWING IN CIRCLES AND GETTING **NOWHERE!** BUT IF YOU DILIGENTLY APPLY **BOTH** OARS AT AN EQUAL AND EVEN PACE **THEN IT WILL WORK FOR YOU!**

PAUL WROTE THAT ONE OF THE MOST IMPORTANT THINGS FOR US TO DO IS **"THE KEEPING OF THE COMMANDMENTS OF GOD"** (1 Corinthians 7:19); BUT GOD ALSO UNDERSTOOD OUR PROPENSITY TO FALL SHORT, SO HE MADE HIS FORGIVING **GRACE** AVAILABLE TO ANY OF THOSE WHO WISH TO ADMIT THEIR SINS AND ASK FORGIVENESS — **"IF ANY MAN SIN, WE HAVE AN ADVOCATE WITH THE FATHER, JESUS CHRIST THE RIGHTEOUS."** (1 John 2:3)

IF "GRACE" IS ALWAYS AVAILABLE, IS IT ALRIGHT TO *IGNORE* GOD'S LAW AND JUST KEEP WILLFULLY *BREAKING IT*? NO, IT IS

NEVER "OK" TO BREAK GOD'S LAW!

THAT'S WHY PAUL WROTE:

"What then? Shall we sin, because we are not under law, but under grace? God forbid!"

Romans 6:15

AND AGAIN I REMIND YOU — "SIN" IS DEFINED AS *"THE TRANSGRESSION OF THE LAW"*!

THE *TRUTH* OF THE MATTER IS THAT FOR ALL OF THOSE WHO TRULY ACCEPT *JESUS* AS THEIR SAVIOR,

THEY WILL FIND OUT THAT IT IS IMPOSSIBLE TO SEPARATE "GOD'S LAW" FROM THE GOSPEL OF JESUS CHRIST!

IS GOD SERIOUS ABOUT THE THINGS THAT HE HAS COMMUNICATED TO US IN THE BIBLE?

YES!

PSALMS 89:34 SAYS, "MY COVENANT WILL I NOT BREAK, NOR ALTER THE THING THAT HAS GONE OUT OF MY LIPS"!

GOD IS *EXTREMELY* SERIOUS ABOUT HIS WORDS!

"For whosoever shall keep the whole law, and yet *offend* in one point, *he is guilty of all!*"

James 2:10

IT'S SIMPLE!

THE VERY NEXT VERSE SHOWS THAT JAMES WAS REFERRING TO THE *10 COMMANDMENTS* — AND HE TOLD US THAT WE ARE COUNTED AS "TRANSGRESSORS" IF WE BREAK EVEN

ONE OF GOD'S LAWS!

THIS IS ABSOLUTE, *DIRECT* COUNSEL TO ALL THE NEW TESTAMENT CHRISTIANS THAT GOD'S LAW IS *100%* INTACT, AND **ALL** OF US ARE EXPECTED TO ACKNOWLEDGE AND OBEY GOD'S LAW!

"Know ye not, that to whom ye yield yourselves servants to obey, his servants ye are to whom ye obey; whether of sin unto *death*, or of obedience unto righteousness?"

Romans 6:16

PART 4

"LEGALISM"

SOME PEOPLE SAY WE SHOULDN'T PUT SO MUCH EMPHASIS ON "THE LAW," AND THAT THOSE WHO DO ARE GETTING INTO **LEGALISM** — BUT THE TRUTH OF THE MATTER IS THAT THERE IS A **HEALTHY** FORM OF **LEGALISM**, AND THERE IS AN UNHEALTHY "EXTREME" FORM OF LEGALISM!

ONE OF PAUL'S VERY CLEAR VERSES STATES ...

" ... I had not known sin, but by _the law_: for I had not known lust, except the _law_ had said, Thou shalt not covet."

Romans 7:7

WHAT IS PAUL SAYING? HE IS SAYING THAT

HE NEEDED TO READ AND UNDERSTAND THE

LAW

OR HE WOULDN'T EVEN KNOW WHAT WAS "SIN"!

THE JEWS OF CHRIST'S DAY HAD GONE TOTALLY OVERBOARD WITH THEIR "ADDITIONAL" LAWS — THEY THOUGHT, "IF 10 ARE GOOD, 1000 IS BETTER!" THEY MADE OBEYING "THE LAW" A TERRIBLE **BURDEN** UPON THEIR PEOPLE!

DOES THIS MEAN THE CHRISTIAN SHOULD **TOSS OUT** THE LAW? **NO WAY** — WE WOULDN'T EVEN KNOW WHAT "SIN" IS WITHOUT THE LAW!

THE LAW AS A "MIRROR"

"For if any be a hearer of the word, and not a doer, he is like unto a man beholding his natural face in a glass: For he beholdeth himself, and goeth his way, and straightway forgetteth what manner of man he was. But whoso looketh into the perfect law of liberty, and continueth therein, he being not a forgetful hearer, but a doer of the work, this man shall be blessed in his deed."

James 1:23-25

GOD HAS ARRANGED IT SO THAT WHEN WE LOOK AT HIS LAW, WE WILL SEE OURSELVES AS **SINNERS**, FILTHY IN OUR SINS — (Isaiah 64:6) — FULL OF FLAWS AND WICKEDNESS! THAT IS THE "NORMAL" CONDITION OF FALLEN MANKIND, NO MATTER **WHO** WE ARE OR HOW NICE WE DRESS, GOD'S "MIRROR" SHOWS OUR **TRUE STATE**!

GOD'S LAW SHOWS US THAT WE NEED A SAVIOR TO RESCUE US FROM THIS SITUATION, AND THE ONLY WAY TO EVER BE "CLEANSED" OF OUR SINS IS TO ACCEPT JESUS CHRIST AS YOUR LORD AND SAVIOR! FIRST WE SEE OURSELVES IN **GOD'S LAW**, AND THEN WE APPROPRIATE **GOD'S SAVING GRACE**!

BEING "COVERED" BY GOD'S GRACE

HOW CAN WE BE BOTH UNDER GOD'S LAW AND "COVERED" BY HIS GRACE? IT SOUNDS LIKE A CONTRADICTION, BUT HERE IS THE SIMPLE WAY TO EXPLAIN IT ALL: WHEN WE ARE "UNDER GRACE" IT IS LIKE BEING UNDER A **PROTECTIVE UMBRELLA** SO WE ARE NO LONGER "*UNDER THE PENALTY OF THE LAW*" —

... BUT IF YOU CHOOSE TO REJECT CHRIST AND STEP OUT FROM UNDER THE "PROTECTIVE COVERING" OF GOD'S GRACE, THEN YOU WOULD AGAIN BE UNDER THE CONDEMNATION OF THE LAW!

THE LAW DOES NOT "VANISH" JUST BECAUSE YOU'RE UNDER GRACE — GOD'S LAW IS **ALWAYS** THERE! ALWAYS!

ALWAYS!

---

* See page 12: <u>Heaven and earth must pass away before God's Law can pass away!</u>

GOD'S LAW

I

THOU SHALT HAVE NO OTHER GODS BEFORE ME.

II

THOU SHALT NOT MAKE UNTO THEE ANY GRAVEN IMAGE, OR ANY LIKENESS OF ANY THING THAT IS IN HEAVEN ABOVE, OR THAT IS IN THE EARTH BENEATH, OR THAT IS IN THE WATER UNDER THE EARTH: THOU SHALT NOT BOW DOWN THYSELF TO THEM, NOR SERVE THEM: FOR I THE LORD THY GOD AM A JEALOUS GOD, VISITING THE INIQUITY OF THE FATHERS UPON THE CHILDREN UNTO THE THIRD AND FOURTH GENERATION OF THEM THAT HATE ME; AND SHEWING MERCY UNTO THOUSANDS OF THEM THAT LOVE ME, AND KEEP MY COMMANDMENTS.

III

THOU SHALT NOT TAKE THE NAME OF THE LORD THY GOD IN VAIN; FOR THE LORD WILL NOT HOLD HIM GUILTLESS THAT TAKETH HIS NAME IN VAIN.

IV

REMEMBER THE SABBATH DAY, TO KEEP IT HOLY. SIX DAYS SHALT THOU LABOUR AND DO ALL THY WORK: BUT THE SEVENTH DAY IS THE SABBATH OF THE LORD THY GOD: IN IT THOU SHALT NOT DO ANY WORK, THOU NOR THY SON, NOR THY DAUGHTER, THY MANSERVANT, NOR THY MAIDSERVANT, NOR THY CATTLE, NOR THY STRANGER THAT IS WITH-IN THY GATES: FOR IN SIX DAYS THE LORD MADE HEAVEN AND EARTH, THE SEA AND ALL THAT IN THEM IS, AND RESTED THE SEVENTH DAY: WHEREFORE THE LORD BLESSED THE SABBATH DAY, AND HALLOWED IT.

V

HONOUR THY FATHER AND THY MOTHER: THAT THY DAYS MAY BE LONG UPON THE LAND WHICH THE LORD THY GOD GIVETH THEE.

VI

THOU SHALT NOT KILL.

VII

THOU SHALT NOT COMMIT ADULTERY.

VIII

THOU SHALT NOT STEAL.

IX

THOU SHALT NOT BEAR FALSE WITNESS AGAINST THY NEIGHBOUR.

X

THOU SHALT NOT COVET THY NEIGHBOUR'S HOUSE; THOU SHALT NOT COVET THY NEIGHBOUR'S WIFE, NOR HIS MANSERVANT, NOR HIS MAIDSERVANT, NOR HIS OX, NOR HIS ASS, NOR ANYTHING THAT IS THY NEIGHBOUR'S.

READ EXODUS 20:3-17

THE LORD'S TEN COMMANDMENTS

"Here is the patience of the saints: here are they that **KEEP** the commandments of God and the faith of Jesus."

Revelation 14:12

PART 5

The Ten Commandments in the New Testament

ALL OF THE TEN COMMANDMENTS WERE REAFFIRMED IN THE NEW TESTAMENT:

The 10 Cs (Exodus 20:3-17)	The New Testament
#1 "Thou shalt have no other gods before me."	#1 "Thou shalt worship the Lord thy God..." Matthew 4:10; Revelation 19:10
#2 "Thou shalt not make unto thee any graven image..."	#2 "Keep yourselves from idols." 1 John 5:21; Acts 17:29
#3 "Thou shalt not take the name of the Lord thy God in vain..."	#3 "That the name of God and His doctrine be not blasphemed." 1 Timothy 6:1
#4 "Remember the Sabbath day to keep it holy..."	#4 "The Sabbath was made for man..." Mark 2:27,28; Colossians 1:16; Hebrews 4:4
#5 "Honour thy father and thy mother..."	#5 "Honour thy father and thy mother." Matthew 19:19; Ephesians 6:1-3.
#6 "Thou shalt not kill."	#6 "Thou shalt not kill." Romans 13:9; James 2:11
#7 "Thou shalt not commit adultery."	#7 "Thou shalt not commit adultery." Matthew 19:18
#8 "Thou shalt not steal."	#8 "Thou shalt not steal." Romans 13:9; Ephesians 4:28
#9 "Thou shalt not bear false witness..."	#9 "Thou shalt not bear false witness." Romans 13:9
#10 "Thou shalt not covet..."	#10 "Thou shalt not covet." Romans 7:7

SO DON'T BE FOOLED — ALL OF THE 10 Cs ARE STILL INTACT! NONE OF THEM HAVE BEEN CANCELED!

PART 6

THE "CONSCIENCE"

THE **CONSCIENCE** IS THE FOREMOST MEDIUM THROUGH WHICH THE **HOLY SPIRIT** WORKS — WHEN WE DO SOMETHING WRONG, "OUR CONSCIENCE BOTHERS US" —

BUT THAT IS NOT ALWAYS TRUE! THE "CONSCIENCE" MUST FIRST BE *PROPERLY EDUCATED* BEFORE IT WILL WORK RIGHT!

IF A PERSON HAS CONSTANTLY BEEN TAUGHT **ERROR**, AND THEY HAVE "BELIEVED" IN THAT ERROR, THIS CAN SILENCE THE WORKING OF GOD'S HOLY SPIRIT!

PEOPLE MIGHT ACTUALLY BELIEVE THAT THEY ARE "DOING RIGHT," WHEN THEY ARE ACTUALLY DOING **WRONG*** — WHICH IS WHY JESUS SAID:

" Not every one that saith unto me, Lord, Lord, shall enter into the kingdom of heaven; but he that doeth _the will_ of my Father which is in heaven. Many will say to me in that day, Lord, Lord, have we not prophesied in thy name? and in thy name have cast out devils? and in thy name done many wonderful works? And then will I profess unto them, I never knew you: depart from me, ye that work iniquity!"

Matthew 7:21-23

THESE PEOPLE "THOUGHT" THEY HAD IT RIGHT — BUT THEY **DID NOT**! THEY USED THEIR FREE WILL TO **OVERRIDE** THE WORKING OF THE HOLY SPIRIT, THEREBY STOPPING THEIR CONSCIENCE FROM WORKING PROPERLY!

WHAT IS GOD'S **WILL** FOR US? SEE PSALM 40:8 — "I delight to do thy will, O my God: yea, thy law is within my heart"!

*Proverb 14:12

WHICH OF THE 4 SETS OF LAWS WAS "NAILED TO THE CROSS"?

The Ceremonial Law

Animal sacrifices and the yearly Sabbaths

EPHESIANS 2:15 **CLEARLY** STATES THAT CHRIST ABOLISHED "*THE LAW OF COMMANDMENTS CONTAINED IN ORDINANCES*,"* SO WHEN THE **LAMB OF GOD** DIED ON THE CROSS, ANIMAL SACRIFICES WERE NO LONGER REQUIRED — AND WHILE MANY CHRISTIANS RECEIVE A BLESSING KEEPING THE SEVEN YEARLY SABBATHS, THESE SABBATHS WERE "SHADOWS" THAT WERE ONLY MANDATORY **BEFORE** THE CROSS! THAT IS WHY PAUL WROTE IN **ROMANS 14:5** THAT CHRISTIANS CAN MAKE UP THEIR OWN MINDS ABOUT KEEPING OR NOT KEEPING THE YEARLY SABBATH DAYS!

* 2nd Chronicles 33:8 says the ordinances were written "*by the hand of Moses,*" not God, which indicates that God did not view them as permanent as the Law He wrote in stone! Also see Colossians 2:14!

THIS IS THE **ONLY** SET OF LAWS THAT CAN LOGICALLY BE "DONE AWAY WITH" AT THE CROSS! **NO MORE** CIRCUMCISION, **NO MORE** ANIMAL SACRIFICES — AND SEEING THAT GENTILES WOULD NOT RELATE TO "COMING OUT OF EGYPT" TO ESCAPE 400 YEARS OF EGYPTIAN CAPTIVITY, GOD DECIDED TO CANCEL THE CEREMONIAL LAW!

PASSOVER, ETC., WOULD MEAN NOTHING TO GENTILE CONVERTS, AND ORDERING THEM TO KEEP THE SEVEN YEARLY SABBATHS WOULD MAKE CHRISTIANS "KEEP TURNING BACK" TO THE JEWISH CULTURE, BUT NOW GOD WISHED FOR THE GOSPEL TO BE **TAKEN TO THE REST OF THE WORLD**, NOT TO THE JEWS.

Acts 13:46

WITH THE POPULARITY OF "MESSIANIC" JUDAISM TODAY, SOME PREFER JUST TO QUOTE COLOSSIANS 2:14 AND BELIEVE THAT THE ONLY THING THAT WAS "*BLOTTED OUT*" WAS THE MERE "*HANDWRITING OF ORDINANCES THAT WAS AGAINST US,*" AS IF THE ONLY THING THAT WAS NAILED TO THE CROSS WAS A **LIST** OF OUR SINS — BUT THAT IGNORES EPHESIANS SAYING THAT "*THE LAW OF COMMANDMENTS*" WAS NAILED TO THE CROSS,

NOT JUST A LIST OF SINS!

THE OTHER **3** SETS OF LAWS REMAIN INTACT ...

The Civil Law	The Moral Law	The Health Law
This law never vanished — that would be saying that society does not need any "rules," which would be ridiculous!	God's Ten Commandments are eternal! "My covenant I will not break, nor alter the thing that is gone out of my lips." Psalms 89:34	Unclean animals are still unclean and forbidden to be eaten! Peter's vision was to show him that **NO MAN** is to be called unclean! Acts 10:10-17, 28

In THE OLD TESTAMENT DAYS THE LORD USED HIS OWN HAND TO WRITE THE **LAW** UPON INANIMATE STONE TABLETS, BUT **NOW** HE DESIRES TO WRITE THEM IN OUR **MINDS** AND INTO OUR **HEARTS** !

Hebrews 10:16

THE HEART IS THE SYMBOL OF **LOVE** —

" *If you love me, keep my commandments.* "

John 14:15, 1 John 5:3

Jesus WANTS US TO **LOVE** GOD'S LAW, *"TAKE IT TO HEART,"* AND USE THIS CONNECTION TO ENABLE GOD'S **GRACE** TO CHANGE OUR LIVES ! THIS IS THE **NEW COVENANT**, THE LAW WRITTEN IN THE HEART !

Hebrews 8:10 + 10:16

30

TRUE LOVE...

JESUS DIED FOR YOUR SINS!

JESUS WENT TO THE CROSS AND HE GAVE HIS LIFE FOR **YOU** — WHY? BECAUSE GOD SAID, "*THE WAGES OF SIN IS DEATH*"!*

ALL OF US HAVE SINNED, AND WE ARE ALL THEREFORE UNDER GOD'S DEATH PENALTY! BUT JESUS WENT TO THE CROSS AND TOOK OUR PENALTY FOR US — AND IF WE ACCEPT HIM AS OUR LORD AND SAVIOR, WE WILL **NOT** HAVE TO EXPERIENCE WHAT THE BIBLE CALLS "*THE SECOND DEATH*"! (Revelation 2:11, 20:6,14, 21:8) BUT THIS ENTAILS OBEYING GOD'S **LAWS**, AND ACCEPTING HIS **GRACE**!

* Genesis 2:17, Romans 6:23, Hebrews 9:27

PART 7 INTER

PASTOR ANDERSON,
I WANT TO THANK YOU
FOR THAT GREAT PRESENTATION
OF THE IMPORTANCE OF *LAW
AND GRACE* —
I THINK YOU MADE IT VERY CLEAR
THAT *GOD'S GRACE* NEVER
ANNULLED OR CANCELLED
GOD'S LAW
WHEN JESUS WENT TO
THE CROSS!

THE *CEREMONIAL LAW*
WAS THE ONLY SET OF LAWS
THAT WAS "NAILED
TO THE CROSS"!

AND GOD'S
GRACE
NEVER
CANCELLED THE
OTHER LAWS,
ESPECIALLY
NOT THE
*TEN
COMMANDMENTS!*

MISSION

THAT'S ABSOLUTELY RIGHT, PASTOR DOUG!

BY THE WAY, A LOT OF PEOPLE HAVE NOTICED THAT YOU AND I LOOK SOMEWHAT *ALIKE* — NOW I WONDER WHAT MIGHT HAVE GIVEN THEM THAT IDEA! *Chuckle*

IT MUST HAVE SOMETHING TO DO WITH OUR HAVING *THE SAME BARBER* — THESE THINGS *HAPPEN* — BUT LET'S GET BACK TO OUR SEMINAR! YOU KNOW, I DO A LOT OF TALKS IN VARIOUS *PRISONS*, AND THOSE PEOPLE WHO ARE IN JAIL *KNOW* THAT "LAWS" ARE *SERIOUS THINGS* — THEY ARE LOCKED UP BECAUSE THEY *BROKE* CERTAIN LAWS! AND EVERY CHRISTIAN NEEDS TO UNDERSTAND THAT THERE'S *NO WAY* THAT "ALL" OF GOD'S LAWS WERE CANCELLED AT THE CROSS OR THAT IT'S "OK" TO BREAK THEM!

PART 8

What are we supposed to "do"?

ROMANS 2:13 TELLS US THAT WE ARE NOT JUST TO BE "HEARERS" OF GOD'S LAW, BUT WE MUST BE **DOERS** OF THE LAW TO BE JUSTIFIED! AND VERSE **15** TELLS US AGAIN THAT GOD WANTS TO WRITE HIS LAW IN OUR HEARTS!

JAMES 2:8 CALLS GOD'S LAW **"THE ROYAL LAW,"** AND HE ALSO CALLED IT **"THE LAW OF LIBERTY"** IN VERSE **12** —

AND I ASSURE YOU, IF EVERYONE FOLLOWED AND OBEYED GOD'S LAWS, THEN THIS WORLD WOULD BE A BEAUTIFUL PLACE!

NO ONE WOULD STEAL, NO ONE WOULD LIE OR COVET OR KILL OR USE GOD'S NAME IN VAIN, ETC., **BECAUSE THEY WOULD FOLLOW GOD'S LAWS!**

GOD'S

I
Thou shall have no other gods before me.
II
Thou shall not make any graven image and bow down to it.

III
Thou shall not take the name of the Lord in vain.

IV
Remember the Sabbath day and keep it holy. Six days shalt thou labor, but the seventh day is the Sabbath of the Lord thy God.

LAW

V
Honor thy father and mother.
VI
Do not kill.
VII
Do not commit adultery.
VIII
Do not steal.
IX
Do not bear false witness.
X
Do not covet thy neighbor's house or his wife, or anything that is thy neighbor's.

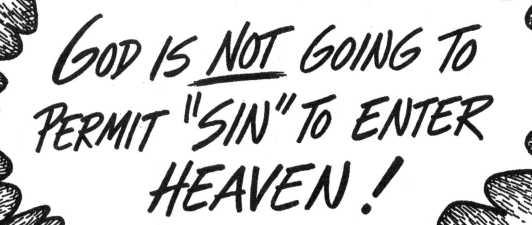

GOD IS <u>NOT</u> GOING TO PERMIT "SIN" TO ENTER HEAVEN !

GOD ABHORS SIN — AND JESUS HAS ABSOLUTELY NO INTENTION OF EVER GOING TO THE CROSS AGAIN ! (Naham 1:9)

THIS MEANS THAT HUMAN BEINGS HAVE TO LEARN TO *OBEY** GOD RIGHT NOW AND RIGHT HERE — *IN THIS WORLD* !

AND THE ONLY WAY THIS HAPPENS IS IF WE ACCEPT AND USE GOD'S GRACE TO EMPOWER US TO BE ABLE TO <u>KEEP</u> GOD'S LAWS !

JESUS WANTS US TO BE "OVERCOMERS" AND TO BE "PERFECT" — AND HE WOULD NOT HAVE SAID THIS UNLESS IT *CAN* HAPPEN !

Revelation 2:7, 3:21, 21:7
Matthew 5:48

* I Samuel 15:22, 2 Cor. 10:5 Isaiah 1:17

PART 9

THE SABBATH

So, IF THE **TEN COMMANDMENTS** WERE NEVER "CANCELLED"...

... WHAT ABOUT THE **7th DAY SABBATH ?**

THE **4th** COMMANDMENT TELLS US TO KEEP THE SABBATH — THE BIBLE SAYS THAT THE **7th DAY*** WAS BLESSED AND SANCTIFIED DURING **CREATION WEEK**, AND **ISAIAH 66:22-23** SAYS THAT **EVERYONE** IN THE "NEW EARTH" WILL BE COMING TO WORSHIP GOD **EVERY SABBATH DAY !**

AND WHICH "SABBATH" DAY WAS ISAIAH REFERRING TO ? HE WAS WRITING ABOUT THE **7th DAY SABBATH**, THE SABBATH THAT GOD GAVE TO MANKIND THE DAY AFTER HE CREATED **ADAM** AND **EVE**, THE SABBATH THAT HE MADE BEFORE MANKIND EVER SINNED !

* THE 7th DAY OF THE WEEK IS SATURDAY

IS THE 7th DAY SABBATH A "JEWISH" THING?

If you think it is, you are about to receive a BIG SURPRISE...

The CHART of

Language/Country	Name of 7th Day
1 Shemitic (Hebrew Bible):	**"Day the Sabbath"**
2 Hebrew (ancient and modern):	**"Shabbath (Sabbath)"**
3 Targum of Onkelos (Hebrew literature):	**"Sabbath"**
4 Targum Dialect of Kurdistan Jews:	**"Holy Sabbath Day"**
5 Ancient Syriac:	**"Shabbatho (Sabbath)"**
6 Chaldee Syriac:	**"Shapta (Sabbath)"**
7 Samaritan (Palestine):	**"Day the Seventh, Sabbath"**
8 Babylonian (Mesopotamia):	**"Sabatu (Sabbath)"**
9 Assyrian (Euphrates and Tigris Valleys):	**"Sabatu (Sabbath)"**
10 Assyrian Planetary Names:	"Saturn"
11 Arabic (very old names):	**"Chief or Rejoicing Day"**
12 Arabic (ancient and modern):	**"Assbat (The Sabbath)"**
13 Maltese (Malta):	**"Issibt (The Sabbath)"**
14 Ethiopic (Abyssinia):	**"Sanbat (Sabbath)"**
15 Tigre (Abyssinia):	**"Sanbat (Sabbath)"**
16 Amharic (Abyssinia):	**"Sanbat (Sabbath)"**
17 Falasha (Jews of Abyssinia):	**"Yini Sanbat (The Sabbath)"**
18 Hamitic (Old Egyptian):	"Saturn"
19 Coptic (dead Egyptian language):	**"Sabbaton (Sabbath)"**
20 Orms or Galla (south of Abyssinia):	**"Zambada (Sabbath)"**
21 Tamashek or Towurek (Africa):	**"Ahalessabt (Sabbath)"**
22 Kabyle or Berber (North Africa):	**"Ghas (Sabbath Day)"**
23 Hausa (Central Africa):	**"Assebatu (Sabbath)"**
24 Japhetic (Sanscrit, India):	"Saturn day"
25 Hindi (India):	"Saturn day"
26 Pali (India):	"Saturn day"
27 Hindustani (India):	**"Shamba (Sabbath day)"**
28 Sindhi (India):	"Saturn"
29 Sindhi Mohammadan:	"Saturn day"
30 Gujarati (India):	"Saturn day"
31 Marathi (India):	"Saturn day"
32 Cashmere (India):	"Idolator's Day"
33 Punjabi (India):	**"Bar (Door or turn Day)"**
34 Punjabi Muhammadan (India):	"Saturn"
35 Bengali (India):	"Saturn day"
36 Assamese (India):	"Saturn day"
37 Uriya (India):	"Saturn day"
38 Afghan (Afghanistan):	**"Shamba (Sabbath)"**
39 Pahlavi (Ancient Persian):	**"Dies Sabbati (Sabbath)"**
40 Persian:	**"Shambtu (Holiday, Sabbath)"**
41 Mythological (Persia):	"Black to Saturn"
42 Armenian:	**"Shapat (Sabbath)"**
43 Kurdish:	**"Shamba (Sabbath)"**
44 Brahuiky (Beluchistan):	**"Shambe (Sabbath)"**
45 Tartaric:	"Saturn day"
46 Sharra (Eastern Mongolia):	**"Bemba (Sabbath)"**
47 Kalmuk (Western Mongolia):	**"Bembe (Center Day)"**
48 Turkish:	**"Yomessabt (Day the Sabbath)"**
49 Laren (Trebizond):	**"Sabbatin (Sabbath)"**
50 Kazani-Tartar (East Russia):	**"Subbota (Sabbath)"**
51 Dravidian (India):	"Saturn day"
52 Malayalam (Inida):	"Saturn day"
53 Kodagu (Southern India):	"Saturn day"
54 Kanarese (India):	"Saturn day"
55 Telugu (India):	"Saturn day"
56 Singhalese (Ceylon):	"Saturn day"
57 Ancient Chinese:	"Saturn"
58 Chinese (Catholic):	**"Chanlitsi (Worship-day 7)"**
59 Chinese (Protestant):	"Worship-day Six"
60 Muhammadan Chinese:	**"Saibitai (Sabbath)"**

THERE ARE _160_ ANCIENT AND MODERN CULTURES THAT HAVE HAD A *7-DAY WEEK* —

AND THERE IS ONLY ONE PLACE A *7-DAY WEEK* COMES FROM! THE *7-DAY WEEK* COMES FROM *GOD'S 7 DAYS OF CREATION WEEK!* DID THE "JEWS" FORCE ALL THESE CULTURES TO KEEP A *7-DAY WEEK*?? NO!

the WEEK

Language/Country	Name of 7th Day
61 Annamite:	**"Ngay Thubay (Day in order Seven)"**
62 Siamese (Siam):	"Day Saturn"
63 Kambojan:	"Day Saturn"
64 Burmese (Burma):	"Saturn"
65 Ancient Peguan:	**"T'pauh (Day Seven)"**
66 Modern Peguan:	"Saturn day"
67 Sban (Burmah):	"Saturn day"
68 Manipuri (south of Assam):	"Saturn"
69 Khassi (east of Bengal):	**"Purification Day"**
70 Ancient Rong (Tibet):	"Earth Planet Day"
71 Modern Rong:	"Planet Saturn"
72 Japanese:	"Saturn day"
73 Corean:	"Saturn"
74 Tibetan (Tibet):	**"Zapenpa (Planet Seven)"**
75 Boutan (Little Tibet):	**"Seventh Brilliant Star"**
76 Georgian (Caucasus):	**"Shabati (Sabbath)"**
77 Suanian (Caucasus):	**"Sammtyn (Sabbath)"**
78 Ingoush (Caucasus):	**"Shatt (Sabbath)"**
79 Avar (Cis-Caucasus):	**"Samatqo (Sabbath Day)"**
80 Circassian:	"Morrow after Assembly"
81 Malayan (Sumatra):	**"Hari Sabtu (Day Sabbath)"**
82 Javanese (Java):	**"Saptoe (Sabbath)"**
83 Sunda (West Java):	**"Saptu (Sabbath)"**
84 Dayak (Borneo):	**"Sabtu (Sabbath)"**
85 Makssar (Salayer Islands):	**"Sattu (Sabbath)"**
86 Bugis:	**"Sattu (Sabbath)"**
87 Malagassy (Madagaskar):	**"Alsabotsy (Sabbath)"**
88 Nuforian (New Guinea):	**"Ras Fiek (Day Seven)"**
89 Swahili (Africa):	**"Assabt (The Sabbath)"**
90 Congo (Africa):	**"Kiansabulu (Sabbath)"**

Language/Country	Name of 7th Day
91 Wolof (West Africa):	**"Alereasser (Sabbath)"**
92 Fulah (West Africa):	**"Essibt (Sabbath)"**
93 Mandigo (West Africa):	**"Aibiti (Sabbath)"**
94 Teda (Central Africa):	**"Essebdu (The Sabbath)"**
95 Bornu (Central Africa):	**"Sibda (Sabbath)"**
96 Fulfude (Central Africa):	**"Assebdu (The Sabbath)"**
97 Sonyal (Central Africa):	**"Assebdu (The Sabbath)"**
98 Logone (Central Africa):	**"Sesibde (The Sabbath)"**
99 Wandala (Central Africa):	**"Sibda (Sabbath)"**
100 Bagrimma (Central Africa):	**"Sibbedt (Sabbath)"**
101 Maba (Central Africa):	**"Sab (Sabbath)"**
102 Norman French (10th century):	**"Sabbedi (Sabbath Day)"**
103 Ancient French (12th century):	**"Samedi (Sabbath Day)"**
104 D'oc. French (ancient and modern):	**"Dissata (Day Sabbath)"**
105 Ecclesiastical (Roman):	**"Sabbatum"**
106 Parliamentary (British):	**"Dies Sabbath"**
107 Astronomical:	"Saturn"
108 Basque (Spain and France):	**"Larumbat"**
109 Finnish (Finland):	**"Lauvantai"**
110 Esthonian (Baltic Russia):	**"Laupaaw (Bath day)"**
111 Livonian (Baltic Russia):	**"Puolpaava (Half day)"**
112 Lap (Norway):	**"Lavardak"**
113 Morduin (Russia):	**"Subbota (Sabbath)"**
114 Tsheremissian (Russia):	**"Kukskeca (No work day)"**
115 Permian (Russia):	**"Subota (Sabbath)"**
116 Votiak (Russia):	**"Subbota (Sabbath)"**
117 Hungarian (Hungary):	**"Szombat (Sabbath)"**
118 Vogul (Russia):	"Xatitkatel (Sixth day)"
119 Ostiac (Russia):	**"Juolynchatl (Hinder end-day)"**
120 Gaelic (Ireland):	"Saturn"

cont'd

108 OF THESE 160 LANGUAGES CALL THE 7th DAY OF THE WEEK THE "SABBATH" DAY OR "REST" DAY !!

Language/Country	Name of 7th Day
121 Welsh (Wales):	"Day Saturn"
122 Cornish (Cornwall):	"Day Saturn"
123 Breton (France):	"Saturn"
124 Greek (Greece):	**"Sabbath"**
125 Modern Greek:	**"Sabbath"**
126 Albanian (Turkish Albania):	"Saturn"
127 Latin (Italy):	**"Sabbtum (Sabbath)"**
128 Italian (Italy):	**"Sabato (Sabbath)"**
129 Spanish (Spain):	**"Sabado (Sabbath)"**
130 Portuguese (Portugal):	**"Sabbado (Sabbath)"**
131 French (France):	**"Samedi (Sabbath Day)"**
132 Roman (Spain):	**"Dissapte (Day Sabbath)"**
133 Rhetian (Switzerland):	"Sonda"
134 Wallachian (Roumania):	**"Sambata (Sabbath)"**
135 Gothic:	"Viko" (name of 7-day week)
136 Old High German:	**"Sambartag (Sabbath's Day)"**
137 Old Low German:	"Wica" (name of 7-day week)
138 Anglo-Saxon (England):	"Saturn's day/Saturday"
139 Friesian (Holland):	"Saterdi/Saturday"
140 High German:	**"Samstag (Sabbath's Day)"**
141 Low German:	"Sunnabend (Sunday's eve)"
142 Dutch (Holland):	"Zaturdag (Saturday)"
143 Modern Frissian (Holland):	"Sniund"
144 English (England):	"Saturday/Saturn's day"
145 Icelandic (Iceland):	**"Laugardagur (of bath day)"**
146 Swedish (Sweden):	**"Lordag (after Laugardagur)"**
147 Danish (Denmark):	**"Laverdag (after Laugardagur)"**
148 Old Slave (Bulgaria):	**"Subbota (Sabbath)"**
149 Russian (Russia):	**"Subbota (Sabbath)"**
150 Illyrian (Servia):	**"Sobota (Sabbath)"**
151 New Slovenian (Austria):	**"Sobota (Sabbath)"**
152 Bulgarian (Bulgaria):	**"Subbota (Sabbath)"**
153 Polish (Poland):	**"Sobota (Sabbath)"**
154 Bohemian (Bohemia):	**"Sobota (Sabbath)"**
155 Lusatian (Saxony):	**"Sobota (Sabbath)"**
156 Polabic (borders of the Elbe):	**"Subuta (Sabbath)"**
157 Lithuanian (Lithuania):	**"Fubata (Sabbath)"**
158 Prussian (Prussia):	**"Sabatico (Sabbath)"**
159 Lettish (Baltic Russia):	"Sesdina (Sixth day)"
160 English Bible:	**"The Seventh Day, The Sabbath"**

108 "7th DAY SABBATHS"!

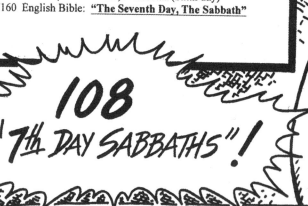

THIS LIST IS **ABSOLUTE PROOF** THAT THE 7th DAY SABBATH IS **NOT** MERELY A "JEWISH" INSTITUTION!

THERE IS **NO WAY** THAT THE JEWISH PEOPLE "CONTROLLED" OR MADE THESE NATIONS TO NAME THEIR **7th DAYS** AFTER THE "JEWISH" SABBATH DAY!

ALL OF THE PEOPLE IN ALL THE NATIONS OF THE WORLD CAN TRACE THEIR HISTORY AND THEIR "ROOTS" BACK TO BEING DISPERSED FROM THE **TOWER OF BABEL**, AND **ALL** OF THOSE ANCIENT PEOPLE KNEW GOD BLESSED THE **7th DAY**!

ISN'T IT INTERESTING HOW **PAGANISM** HAS WORKED ITS WAY INTO VARIOUS CULTURES SO THAT PEOPLE DECIDED TO "IGNORE" GOD AND START NAMING THE DAYS OF THE WEEK AFTER **MYTHS** OF "THOR" AND THE "MOON" DAY AND THE "SUN" DAY AND THE PLANET **SATURN**, "SATURDAY" — BUT THE **TRUTH** IS STILL THERE IN **108** CULTURES!

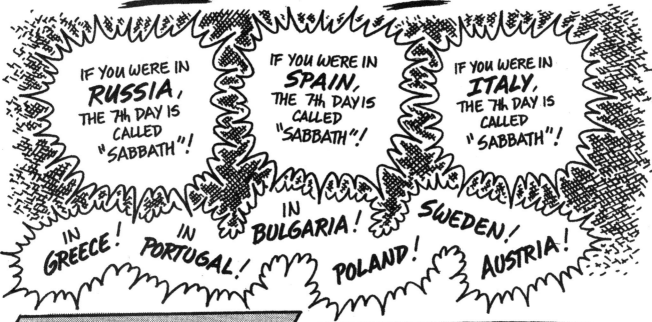

IF YOU WERE IN **RUSSIA**, THE 7th DAY IS CALLED "SABBATH"!

IF YOU WERE IN **SPAIN**, THE 7th DAY IS CALLED "SABBATH"!

IF YOU WERE IN **ITALY**, THE 7th DAY IS CALLED "SABBATH"!

IN **GREECE**!   IN **PORTUGAL**!   **BULGARIA**!   **SWEDEN**!   **POLAND**!   **AUSTRIA**!

So, WHAT ABOUT **AMERICA**?

AMERICA USES THE PAGAN "SATURDAY" NAME FOR ITS **7th** DAY OF THE WEEK — OUR "SATURN-DAY" WAS PASSED ONTO US FROM THE ANGLO-SAXON CULTURE OF **ENGLAND**, WHICH SEEMS TO INDICATE THAT THOSE FOLKS CHOSE TO PAY A BIT TOO MUCH ATTENTION TO THE **DRUIDS** WHO BUILT **STONEHENGE**! THEY CHOSE TO IGNORE THE GOD OF THE BIBLE —

INTERESTING NOTE :

THE CHART OF THE WEEK (WHICH HAS ONLY BEEN PARTIALLY REPRODUCED HERE) WAS PUT TOGETHER OVER 100 YEARS AGO BY _DR. WILLIAM MEADE JONES,_ A WELL-KNOWN RESEARCH EXPERT WHO LIVED IN _LONDON, ENGLAND!_

FOR A FULL CHART, CONTACT _AMAZING FACTS —_

BEWARE OF FALSE DOCTRINES!

"Amazing" Statistics ....

Adriatic Union: **98**
Africa (Central): **739**
Africa (East): **2,135**
Africa (Southern): **670**
Africa (West): **626**
Angola: **556**
Asia (Southwest): **286**
Austral (S. Am.): **454**
Australia: **188**
Austria: **44**

Baltic Union: **73**
Bangladesh: **92**
Bolivia: **223**
Botswana: **51**
Brazil: **3,140**
Bulgaria: **77**
Burundi: **123**

Canada: **333**
Caribbean: **500**
Central America: **1,227**
Central Pacific: **221**
Czechoslovakia: **176**
Chile: **451**
China: **824**
Columbia: **777**
Congo: **1,083**
Cuba Union: **189**

Denmark: **49**
Dominican Union: **482**

Ecuador: **68**
England: **210**
Ethiopia: **686**
Europe (Southeast): **200**

Finland: **69**
France: **139**
French Antilles: **116**

Germany: **592**
Guam-Micronesia: **18**

Hatian Union: **327**
Hungary: **108**

India (Central): **391**
India (Northeast): **141**
India (Northern): **168**
India (South): **487**
Indian Ocean: **289**
Indonesia (East): **567**
Indonesia (West): **582**
Italy: **88**

Japan: **115**

Korea: **678**

Malawi: **557**
Mexico (North): **473**
Mexico (South): **1,185**
Middle East: **68**
Mongolia: **1**
Mozambique: **735**
Myanmar (near Laos): **183**

Netherlands: **48**
Nigeria: **600**
Norway: **72**

Pakistan: **73**
Papua New Guinea: **727**
Peru: **1,110**
Philippines (Central): **996**
Philippines (North): **1,251**
Philippines (South): **1,589**
Poland: **123**
Portugal: **77**
Puerto Rico: **260**

Romania: **973**
Russia (East): **139**
Russia (Moldova): **127**
Russia (Southern): **105**
Russia (Ukraine): **711**
Russia (West): **449**
Rwanda: **865**

Spain: **58**
Sri Lanka: **31**
Sweden: **46**
Switzerland: **56**

Tanzania: **964**
Trans Tasman: **306**

Uganda: **651**
United States: **4,470**

Venezuela: **446**

West Indies: **599**
Western Pacific: **220**

Zaire: **1,105**
Zambia: **1,630**

AS YOU ALL KNOW, PASTOR DOUG AND I ARE **SEVENTH-DAY ADVENTISTS**, AND I THINK IT'S IMPORTANT FOR EVERYONE TO BE AWARE OF HOW THE LORD HAS BLESSED THIS WONDERFUL MOVEMENT! THE ADVENTIST CHURCH WAS FOUNDED IN THE **1860s**, AND IT NOW HAS MORE CHURCHES IN MORE COUNTRIES THAN ANY OTHER PROTESTANT CHURCH!

ADVENTISTS HAVE **47,543** CHURCHES IN **209** COUNTRIES!

WHICH PROVES THAT THE TRUTH ABOUT THE **7th DAY SABBATH** OF THE LORD'S TEN COMMANDMENTS IS STILL KNOWN AROUND THE WORLD!

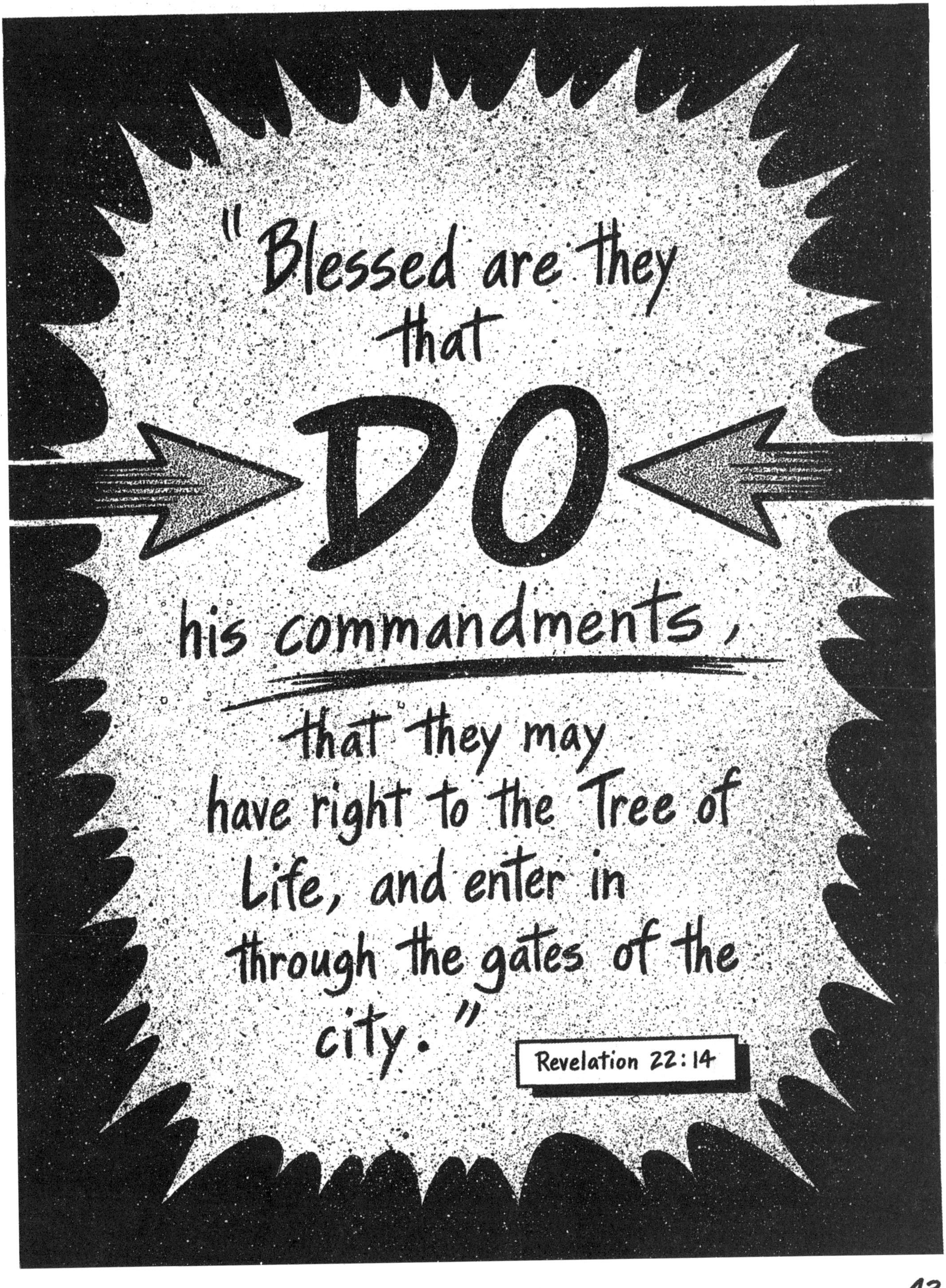

"Blessed are they that

DO

his commandments,

that they may have right to the Tree of Life, and enter in through the gates of the city."

Revelation 22:14

ROMANS 3:19
TELLS US
THAT THE
LAW
SHALL JUDGE
THE
WHOLE
WORLD!

Psalms 96:13
1 John 5:19

GOD'S LAW

WHICH "LAW"?

THE ONE THAT GOD WROTE IN STONE, AND THE OTHERS THAT MOSES WROTE "IN A BOOK" (Deut. 31:24) WHICH WERE NOT "NAILED TO THE CROSS"!

"The Law is holy, and the commandment holy, and just, and good!"

Romans 7:12

"For I delight in the Law of God...!"

Romans 7:22

THIS DESERVES TO BE **REPEATED**...
JUST HOW "IMPORTANT" IS GOD'S TEN COMMANDMENT LAW ?...

THIS IS THE **BIBLE'S** DEFINITION OF "SIN":

" SIN IS THE TRANSGRESSION OF THE LAW "!!

I John 3:4

ALL OF US ARE SINNERS, AND **ALL** OF US ARE "GUILTY" OF **BREAKING GODS LAWS**!

Romans 3:23

"... Where no law is, there is no transgression."

Romans 4:15

— BUT WE **ARE** SINNERS, SO THE LAW EXISTS.!!

GUILTY!

AND WHAT IS THE **ONE THING** THAT IS MORE POWERFUL THAN THE **LAW** ?... **GOD'S GRACE!** ...BUT ONLY IF YOU ACCEPT IT.!

SATAN HATES GOD'S LAW!

THE DEVIL REALLY ENJOYS SEEING PEOPLE TWISTING PAUL'S WRITINGS "UNTO THEIR OWN DESTRUCTION"! IF WE RUN AROUND THINKING THAT THERE'S "NO NEED" TO PAY ATTENTION TO OR "OBEY" GOD'S LAWS, THEN THE DEVIL HAS **WON**!

IT'S YOUR CHOICE

SATAN HAS SPENT THE PAST **6,000 YEARS** LOOKING FOR WAYS TO GET PEOPLE TO "BREAK GOD'S LAWS" — HE LOVES TO SEE US **SIN** AND **KEEP SINNING**! AND THE ONLY WAY THAT OUR SELF-INDULGENT FALLEN NATURES WILL OVERCOME SIN IS FOR US TO **PAY ATTENTION** TO THE REQUIREMENTS OF **GOD'S LAW** AND THEN WE ASK GOD TO GIVE US THE POWER TO **STOP** SINNING!

46

EVERY "SIN" IS A **WILLFUL CHOICE** — AND EVEN "LITTLE WHITE LIES" ARE NOT ACCEPTABLE TO GOD! THIS IS THE THING, GOD'S STANDARDS ARE **EXTREMELY HIGH STANDARDS**!

HERE'S HOW "SIN" HAPPENS:

SIN STARTS AS AN **EVIL IDEA**, A "THOUGHT" THAT POPS INTO OUR HEADS. IF WE **DWELL UPON IT**, AND THEN **ACT UPON IT**, THEN YOU'VE GOT **TROUBLE**!

THE ONLY WAY TO BREAK THIS BEHAVIOR PATTERN IS TO **STOP** THE THOUGHT WHEN IT HAPPENS BY **REPLACING IT** WITH SOMETHING ELSE WHILE **IMMEDIATELY** ASKING GOD FOR HIS HELP! IF THE SIN HAS SOMETHING TO DO WITH "WHERE" YOU ARE, THEN **GET OUT OF THERE**! GET TO A PLACE THAT FEELS "SAFE," AND THEN FIND SOME **GOOD** THINGS TO OCCUPY YOURSELF WITH!

IS IT A "SIN" TO BE TEMPTED?

NO! THIS WILL HAPPEN, BUT WHEN THOSE "IDEAS" POP INTO OUR MINDS WE MUST IMMEDIATELY RECOGNISE THEM AS WRONG AND **REJECT** THEM! MEMORIZING BIBLE VERSES IS THE BEST WAY TO FILL YOUR MIND WITH "GODLY" THOUGHTS!

Psalm 119:11, Philippians 4:8

47

CONCLUSION

AMAZING FACTS

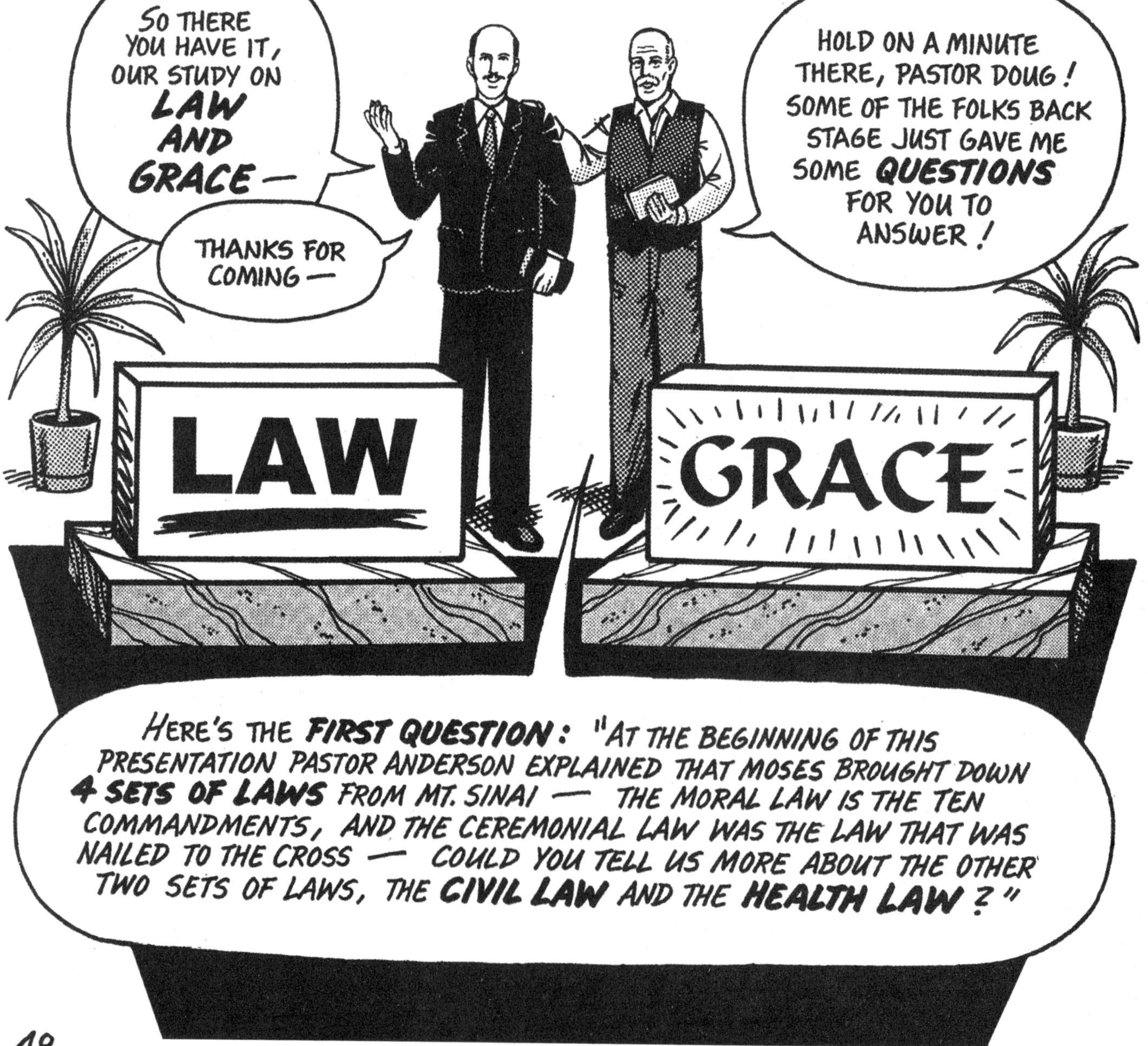

A Quick Word about the DIETARY LAW

THE DIET FOR ADAM AND EVE IN THE GARDEN OF EDEN WAS *FRUIT* AND *NUTS*, THEN *VEGETABLES* WERE ADDED LATER — AND THIS WILL BE THE DIET FOR ALL OF THE REDEEMED IN THE NEW EARTH! MEAT EATING WILL *END* — ANIMALS WILL NEVER AGAIN BE KILLED FOR FOOD! THERE WILL BE *NO MORE DEATH!* (Revelation 21:4)

GOD GAVE MANKIND PERMISSION TO EAT "MEAT" ONLY *AFTER* THE FLOOD (ALL THE VEGETATION WAS DESTROYED), BUT GOD TOLD NOAH THAT SOME ANIMALS WERE *CLEAN*, AND SOME WERE *UNCLEAN* — AND NO ONE WAS TO EAT ANY OF THE *UNCLEAN* ANIMALS! WHY? BECAUSE MOST OF THOSE ANIMALS ARE THE WORLD'S "GARBAGE DISPOSALS"!

THEIR METABOLISMS JUST DON'T PROVIDE THE HEALTHIEST NUTRITION, SO GOD SAID, "DO NOT EAT THEM!"

SOME THINK THAT THE UNCLEAN ANIMALS SHOULD ONLY BE AVOIDED BY *JEWS* — BUT WAS *NOAH* A JEW? *ABRAHAM* WAS THE FIRST "JEW" — SO WHAT ABOUT ALL THE PEOPLE WHO LIVED BEFORE ABRAHAM??

WE ARE ON OUR WAY TO HEAVEN, AND GOD WANTS US CLEAR-MINDED AND HEALTHY —

THAT MEANS IT'S TIME TO START LIVING RIGHT AND EATING THE PROPER FOODS, WHICH MEANS *AVOIDING* ALL OF THE UNCLEAN FOODS MENTIONED IN THE BIBLE!

AMAZING FACTS HAS SEVERAL PAMPHLETS THAT EXPLAIN THE CLEAN AND UNCLEAN ANIMALS — FEEL FREE TO CONTACT US AND ASK ABOUT THEM!

www.amazingfacts.org

UNCLEAN

Pig
Lobster
Catfish
Crabs
Shrimp
Oyster
Clam
Snails

Genesis 1:29; Leviticus 11, Deuteronomy 14, Genesis 7:2, 9:3, Isaiah 66:15-17!

THE **TORAH** CONTAINS A TOTAL OF **613** LAWS, AND THE **CIVIL LAW** DEALS WITH THE "SECULAR" RULES FOR THE SMOOTH RUNNING OF THE ANCIENT JEWISH SOCIETY — AFTER ALL, ACCIDENTS ARE GOING TO HAPPEN, AND CERTAIN CRIMES WILL ALSO TAKE PLACE — AND GOD LISTED A NUMBER OF EXAMPLES OF THOSE EVENTS AND HE TOLD MOSES WHAT WOULD BE THE VARIOUS PENALTIES FOR THOSE CRIMES! THE LIST DOES NOT COVER **ALL** THE POSSIBLE CRIMES, BUT IT PROVIDES A "GUIDE" TO HELP A SOCIETY TO ORGANIZE A FAIR AND EQUITABLE LEGAL SYSTEM!

THE **CIVIL LAWS** LISTED IN THE TORAH HAVE FORMED THE BASIS FOR ALL THE CIVIL LAWS THAT HAVE BEEN PUT IN PLACE IN **EVERY** CITY, **EVERY** TOWN, **EVERY** STATE, AND *EVERY NATION IN THE WORLD!*

ACCORDINGLY, THE **CIVIL LAW** IN THE OLD TESTAMENT TORAH WAS *NEVER* "NAILED TO THE CROSS"!

CIVIL LAWS EXIST TO KEEP THE UNCONVERTED LAW-BREAKERS IN SOCIETY **UNDER CONTROL**, BECAUSE GOD WANTS OUR WORLD *TO BE AS PEACEFUL AS POSSIBLE!*

GOOD ANSWER, PASTOR DOUG!

THE BIBLE TELLS US THAT WE SHOULD STUDY TO SHOW OURSELVES APPROVED OF GOD, "RIGHTLY DIVIDING THE WORD OF TRUTH" (2 Timothy 2:15) — AND THAT IS WHAT WE MUST DO, A DILIGENT STUDY OF THE BIBLE TO UNDERSTAND **GOD'S LAW** AND **GOD'S GRACE** !

GOD LOVES US !

"For by grace are ye saved through faith; and that not of yourselves: it is the gift of God, not of works, lest any man should boast."

Ephesians 2:8,9

WHILE WE ARE NOT SAVED BY OUR "WORKS," THERE _IS_ A "WORK" FOR US TO DO SO THAT WE MIGHT KNOW THE **TRUTH** ABOUT THE VARIOUS DOCTRINES OF THE BIBLE — AFTER ALL, GOD DISAPPROVES OF "LUKEWARM" OR LAZY CHRISTIANS !

WE NEED TO REJOICE AND THANK THE LORD THAT HE HAS SAVED US BY HIS GRACE !

PRAISE THE LORD !

Meekness

"Now the man Moses was very _meek_..."

Numbers 12:3

" The meek will he guide in judgment, and the meek will he teach his way."

Psalms 25:9

"...He will beautify the _meek_ with salvation."

Psalms 149:4

" Blessed are the _meek_, for they shall inherit the earth!"

Matthew 5:5

GOD'S **GRACE** IS THE SOURCE OF REDEEMED'S "MEEKNESS," AND THAT GRACE IS LINKED TO THE **POWER** THAT CREATED AND SUSTAINS THE ENTIRE UNIVERSE — AND THAT POWER IS ALSO FOUND IN THE "LAWS" THAT HOLD TOGETHER **GOD'S UNIVERSE**! IT'S A "PACKAGE DEAL" YOU MIGHT SAY — <grin> —

" For I am meek and lowly in heart."

Matthew 11:29

THIS IS HOW JESUS DESCRIBED HIMSELF, AND WE SHOULD CONSIDER JESUS AS OUR "IDEAL ROLE MODEL"!

ETERNAL LIFE AWAITS THOSE WHO ARE WILLING TO ACCEPT **GOD'S LAWS** AS THE TRUTH THAT BINDS THE UNIVERSE, AND **GOD'S GRACE** IS AVAILABLE TO ALL WHO TRULY WISH TO GET RIGHT WITH GOD — AND THEN THOSE PEOPLE WILL EMBODY A FORM OF **MEEKNESS** THAT HAS THE POWER OF GOD THAT ENABLES ALL OF US TO BECOME **OVERCOMERS**!

Righteousness by Faith

Hebrews 11:6

"Without faith it is impossible to please God."

HOW DO WE GO ABOUT ACCEPTING GOD'S GRACE? WE DO IT BY PLACING OUR **FAITH** IN GOD AND **TRUSTING** HIM AND **BELIEVING** THE PROMISES THAT ARE IN THE BIBLE! "If we confess our sins, He is faithful and just to forgive us our sins, and to cleanse us from all unrighteousness." I John 1:9

THAT'S THE WAY IT'S BEEN DONE THROUGHOUT THE CENTURIES — WE REALIZE OUR NEED FOR GOD, AND WE ACCEPT JESUS AS OUR SAVIOR!

AND THEN IT BECOMES A DAILY PROCESS OF GROWING IN THE LORD AND LIVING BY GODLY STANDARDS — TURNING FROM SIN — AND BECOMING "A NEW CREATURE" IN CHRIST JESUS, AS IT SAYS IN 2nd Corinthians 5:17.

DOES IT WORK? **YES IT DOES!** BUT YOU'LL NEVER KNOW UNLESS YOU **TRY IT!**

HOW SHOULD WE LIVE OUR LIVES?

1. Trust in God and accept Jesus as your Savior!

2. Repent of your sins, confess them to God, and ask Him to rehabilitate you!

3. Have faith in God that He _will_ help you!

4. Educate your conscience so that you will _really_ know what is "right" and "wrong"!

5. Accept that Law and Grace go hand-in-hand!

6. Endure in your faith until the end!

Matthew 24:13

IF YOU TURN YOUR LIFE OVER TO GOD WITH YOUR WHOLE HEART, I PROMISE YOU THAT GOD WILL BE FAITHFUL AND SHOW YOU THAT HE TRULY CARES ABOUT YOU!

AMEN TO THAT, PASTOR DOUG!